# AMERICA AT WAR

# VIETNAM WAR
## 1954-1975

**Simon Rose**

www.av2books.com

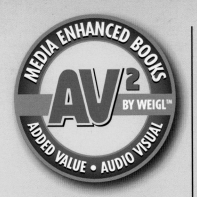

AV² provides enriched content that supplements and complements this book. Weigl's AV² books strive to create inspired learning and engage young minds in a total learning experience.

## Your AV² Media Enhanced books come alive with...

**Audio**
Listen to sections of the book read aloud.

**Key Words**
Study vocabulary, and complete a matching word activity.

**Video**
Watch informative video clips.

**Quizzes**
Test your knowledge.

Go to **www.av2books.com**, and enter this book's unique code.

## BOOK CODE

### D 9 1 4 4 5

**Embedded Weblinks**
Gain additional information for research.

**Slide Show**
View images and captions, and prepare a presentation.

**AV² by Weigl** brings you media enhanced books that support active learning.

**Try This!**
Complete activities and hands-on experiments.

**... and much, much more!**

Published by AV² by Weigl
350 5th Avenue
New York, NY 10118

Website: www.av2books.com        www.weigl.com

Library of Congress Cataloging-in-Publication Data

Rose, Simon, 1961-
Vietnam / Simon Rose.
    pages cm. -- (America at war)
Includes index.
ISBN 978-1-62127-655-5 (hardcover : alk. paper) -- ISBN 978-1-62127-656-2 (softcover : alk. paper)
1. Vietnam War, 1961-1975--Juvenile literature. 2. Vietnam War, 1961-1975--United States--Juvenile literature. I. Title.
DS558.R66 2014
959.704'3--dc23

                        2013001857

Printed in the United States of America in North Mankato, Minnesota
1 2 3 4 5 6 7 8 9 0  17 16 15 14 13

052013
WEP040413

Editor: Heather Kissock
Design: Mandy Christiansen

Photograph Credits
We acknowledge Getty Images, Alamy, and Newscom as our primary photo suppliers.

Every reasonable effort has been made to trace ownership and to obtain permission to reprint copyright material. The publishers would be pleased to have any errors or omissions brought to their attention so that they may be corrected in subsequent printings.

# CONTENTS

# America at War

The United States is a country that was born out of conflict. The American Revolutionary War was a fight for independence from **colonial rule**. From 1776 to 1783, colonists fought British rule for the right to forge their own destiny. Their commitment to the cause established the country as a fierce and loyal **ally**. When called upon, the United States has always fought bravely to protect its values and way of life.

Since its inception, the United States has been involved in a number of wars and conflicts. These include the War of 1812, the U.S. Civil War, the Mexican-American War, and several battles with American Indians. The United States was also involved in the latter stages of World War I and played a major role in World War II. Since 1945 alone, the United States has taken part in conflicts in Korea, Vietnam, Iraq, and Afghanistan.

Navy patrol boats traveled the waterways of Vietnam. They carried supplies to troops stationed inland and also monitored the area for enemy activity.

The Vietnam War was the first war to use helicopters on a large scale. It is sometimes referred to as the Helicopter War as a result.

No matter how a war ends, it usually leads to changes for both sides of the conflict. On the global scale, borders change, new countries are created, people win their freedom, and **dictators** are deposed. Changes also occur on a national level for almost every country involved,

The United States has experienced great change as a result of war. War has shaped the country's political, economic, and social landscapes, making it the country it is today.

# A War Begins

For many years, Vietnam was part of the colonial **empire** of France. During World War II, however, the country was occupied by Japanese forces. Stifled by the occupation, the Vietnamese **communists**, led by Ho Chi Minh, fought the Japanese to become an independent country. When the war ended and the Japanese army retreated, the French returned to reclaim their territory. By this time, Ho Chi Minh and his Viet Minh party had set up their own government and were eager to cut ties with France. The country was soon engaged in a violent conflict.

Ultimately, the French lost the battle and pulled out of Vietnam in 1954. To give politicians time to determine the fate of Vietnam, a temporary settlement was put into effect. Vietnam was divided into two states. North Vietnam became a communist state. A non-communist state was set up in the south. This division was to remain in effect until 1956, when a more permanent decision would be made. However, the election that was to decide the fate of Vietnam was not held, and the country remained divided.

The United States was nervous about the power the communists held in North Vietnam and the influence the north had on the south. It was not willing to let North Vietnam assume control of the south. The United States began supplying South Vietnam with weapons, equipment, and military advisors in an effort to exert its own control in the south. As it sought to gain more control over the situation in Vietnam, the United States became embroiled in the politics of South Vietnam, which were increasingly volatile. In 1963, it indicated its support for a **regime change** in South Vietnam and did nothing to stop a military coup that saw Ngo Dinh Diem, the president of South Vietnam, ousted from office by his own generals.

John F. Kennedy was the U.S. president when Ngo Dinh Diem was removed from office. In the weeks leading up to the coup, President Kennedy met often with key advisors, including U.S. Army Chief of Staff General Maxwell Taylor and Secretary of Defense Robert McNamara, to determine the best course of action for the United States.

# Roots of U.S. Involvement in Vietnam

## THE COLD WAR

Even though the United States and the **Soviet Union** had been allies during World War II, they quickly parted ways afterwards, beginning a conflict now known as the **Cold War**. One of the main reasons for the tension between the two countries was their differing politics. The Soviet Union was a communist state. The United States was **democratic**. Each country lent its support to countries that shared its politics. During the Vietnam conflict, the Soviet Union supported and provided resources for the north. The United States did the same for the south.

## THE TRUMAN DOCTRINE

The United States believed that it had a right and an obligation to support other democratic countries. This belief was stated in a document called the Truman Doctrine. Developed in 1947 by President Harry Truman, the Truman Doctrine was one of the United States' responses to the Soviet threat during the Cold War. The policy allowed the United States to intervene in international conflicts that threatened the freedom of a country's peoples. The United States believed that a threat to democracy in any part of the world was a threat to its own freedoms.

## THE DOMINO THEORY

In 1949, China was overtaken by communist rule. The United States lost a powerful ally and was determined to prevent any further expansion of communism in Asia. It believed that the fall of **Indochina** could lead to the toppling of neighboring countries, such as Thailand, Burma, and the Philippines. This belief was known as the domino theory. To stop the spread of communism in Asia, the United States helped France in its fight against the Viet Minh and supported the non-communist government in South Vietnam after the French left.

## U.S. INTERVENTION

Even though South Vietnam had the support of the United States, it was unable to build its military to a strength that could overpower the north. Communist forces within South Vietnam—called the Viet Cong—were fighting on behalf of Ho Chi Minh to defeat the south and bring it under communist control. The U.S. became concerned about a possible communist takeover. The government increased its aid to South Vietnam and stationed a stronger military presence in the region. By 1963, there were approximately 16,000 U.S. troops in South Vietnam.

# A Global War

**Dwight Eisenhower**
**President of the United States**
**(1953–1961)**

**John F. Kennedy**
**President of the United States**
**(1961–1963)**

**Lyndon B. Johnson**
**President of the United States**
**(1963–1969)**

**Richard Nixon**
**President of the United States**
**(1969–1974)**

**Gerald Ford**
**President of the United States**
**(1974–1977)**

The Vietnam War never reached the status of a world war. In many ways, it remained a civil war between North and South Vietnam. However, the cooperation and participation of key world powers elevated this war beyond its roots. The Vietnam War became a focal point for the conflict between the democratic United States and the communist Soviet Union. When China joined the conflict on the communist side, the threat of a world war became very real.

The map to the right shows the countries and key leaders that were directly involved in the Vietnam War.

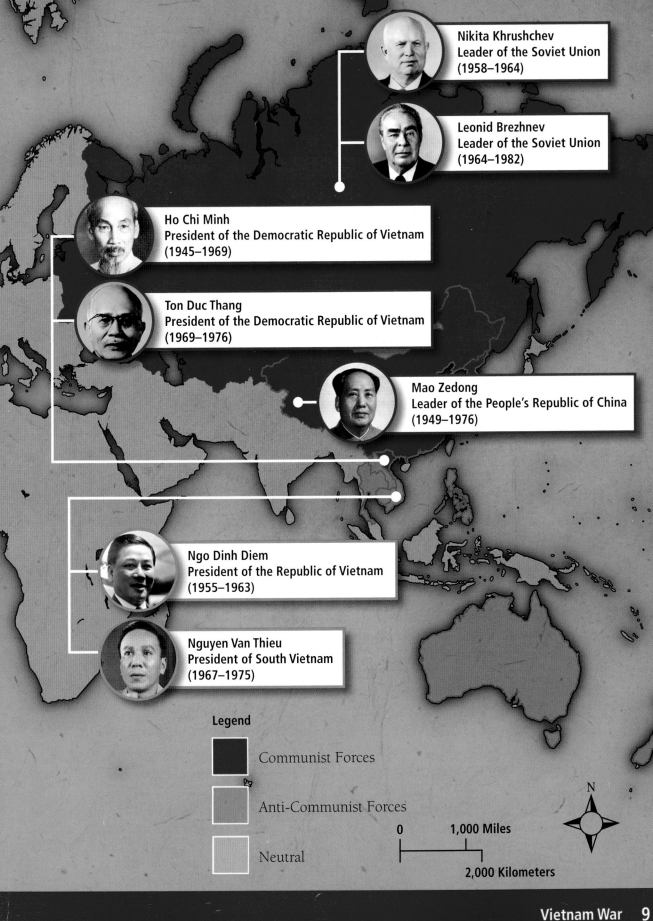

Nikita Khrushchev
Leader of the Soviet Union
(1958–1964)

Leonid Brezhnev
Leader of the Soviet Union
(1964–1982)

Ho Chi Minh
President of the Democratic Republic of Vietnam
(1945–1969)

Ton Duc Thang
President of the Democratic Republic of Vietnam
(1969–1976)

Mao Zedong
Leader of the People's Republic of China
(1949–1976)

Ngo Dinh Diem
President of the Republic of Vietnam
(1955–1963)

Nguyen Van Thieu
President of South Vietnam
(1967–1975)

Legend

Communist Forces

Anti-Communist Forces

Neutral

0    1,000 Miles

2,000 Kilometers

N

# The United States Enters the War

The removal of President Ngo Dinh Diem from office started a chain of events that would bring the Vietnam conflict to a head. On November 2, 1963, one day after being forced from office, Diem was assassinated. The killing made the situation in Vietnam even more precarious. For a while, the government was unstable, as one general after another took over. None of them, however, were able to maintain control of the country. As the threat of a communist takeover grew, U.S. President Lyndon B. Johnson saw no option but to send more military support to South Vietnam.

The increased U.S. presence brought a swift reaction from North Vietnam. On August 2, 1964, North Vietnamese torpedo boats attacked a U.S. Navy destroyer in the Gulf of Tonkin, off the coast of North Vietnam. Two days later, it was reported that the North Vietnamese Navy had launched another attack against U.S. destroyers. In response, President Johnson ordered the bombing of targets in North Vietnam. The attack also led to the U.S. Congress passing the Gulf of Tonkin Resolution.

The United States sent troops and equipment from every arm of the military, including the Navy, Marines, and Air Force.

This gave President Johnson the authority to increase U.S. military involvement in the war in Vietnam. In early 1965, the United States began a bombing campaign, called Operation Rolling Thunder, against targets in North Vietnam. The campaign would continue for almost four years. In March 1965, 3,500 U.S. Marines were sent to Vietnam. Many people supported Johnson's decision at the time, but the war would soon become very unpopular in the United States.

By June 1965, approximately 82,000 American combat troops were stationed in Vietnam. Johnson authorized more troops in July, and by the end of the year, there were approximately 200,000 U.S. military personnel serving in Vietnam. The United States was supported by some of its allies. Australia, New Zealand, the Philippines, South Korea, and Thailand also sent troops to fight in South Vietnam, although on a much smaller scale than the United States.

# Lyndon B. Johnson
# The 36th U.S. President

Lyndon Baines Johnson was born in Texas in 1908. His family was not wealthy, and Johnson had to work his way through university. Initially a schoolteacher, he later turned to politics and was elected to the House of Representatives in 1937. After fighting in World War II, he returned to politics and was elected to the U.S. Senate in 1948. In 1960, he was asked to be John F. Kennedy's running mate and was elected vice president on that ticket. When Kennedy was assassinated in 1963, Johnson immediately became president of the United States.

Johnson was responsible for several social reforms during his presidency. Johnson signed the **Civil Rights Act** into law in July 1964. He also introduced reforms in health, education, housing, transportation, and more laws on civil rights. Johnson was elected as president in 1964. By this time, the United States was already supplying military help to South Vietnam. In 1965, President Johnson increased military support and sent in more U.S. troops.

The war continued with no victory in sight, and by 1968, there was great opposition to U.S. involvement in Vietnam. Johnson had also become very unpopular. In March 1968, Johnson announced that he would not run for re-election as president. He spent much of his remaining time in office working on a peaceful solution to the war in Vietnam. Peace talks began, but the fighting continued. In 1969, Richard Nixon succeeded Johnson as president. On January 22, 1973, Johnson died at his ranch in Texas. The last U.S. combat troops left Vietnam in March 1973.

To show support for the troops, President Johnson visited Vietnam in 1966.

President Johnson and his wife, Lady Bird, spent much of their spare time at the LBJ Ranch in Texas. The ranch was where President Johnson was born, and it is where he died.

# Americans Who Served in Vietnam

The U.S. military possesses a wide range of people who fill a variety of roles. The men and women who served in Vietnam came from various cultural and socio-economic backgrounds and were members of every division of the country's armed forces. Pilots of planes and helicopters came from both the Air Force and Navy. The Navy's sailors served on U.S. ships and aircraft carriers off the coast of Vietnam. Ground soldiers were members of either the U.S. Army or the Marines. Most of the women who served in the war were Army nurses, but some also served in other branches of the armed forces or in non-military organizations.

## Soldiers and Marines

Ground forces made up the majority of U.S. troops fighting in Vietnam. **Infantry** and **artillery** units from the U.S. Army fought alongside Marines and Airborne divisions. The soldiers rarely went into battle against the enemy in a traditional fight. There were no front lines and few direct battles. U.S. troops fought a **guerilla war** in the jungle, mostly against the communist Viet Cong. The communists knew the area very well and were supplied with weapons by North Vietnam. The Viet Cong had hiding places in the jungle and could escape through underground tunnels. In many villages, members of the Viet Cong were able to blend in with the local residents. It was often difficult for U.S. soldiers to know exactly who the enemy was.

Ground soldiers experienced the war up close, often having to travel directly through the devastation on their way to the next battle zone.

## Pilots

Air Force and Navy pilots both played an important role in the war in Vietnam. The Navy's pilots operated from aircraft carriers based in the South China Sea off the coast of Vietnam. They took part in bombing missions against enemy positions and provided support for ground troops.

During the war, the U.S. Air Force operated 10 air bases in South Vietnam. Like their Navy counterparts, Air Force pilots supported troops on the ground. They also carried out close air support for other aircraft, escorted helicopters on their missions, and attacked enemy targets that were close to the battlefields.

U.S. Air Force pilots used a range of aircraft in Vietnam. While helicopters and bombers are the best known, transport planes also played a key role. They were used to drop paratroopers into key battle areas.

Pilots flew helicopters on a variety of combat missions. They also assisted with medical evacuations, flying wounded soldiers from the battlefields to hospitals in South Vietnam. Helicopter pilots played a large role in Operation Frequent Wind on April 29, 1975. This was a massive airlift, during which more than 1,000 U.S. **civilians** and almost 6,000 South Vietnamese refugees were flown out of the capital city of Saigon as the Vietnam War came to an end.

## CHEMICAL WARFARE

Soldiers were constantly under the threat of chemical warfare that the U.S. military used against the enemy. As the Viet Cong hid in the jungle, the United States decided to use chemicals, such as Agent Orange, to destroy all vegetation in the forest. The enemy would then have few places to hide. The chemicals were sprayed on the jungle from helicopters and planes, covering everything in their wake. People who came in contact with the chemicals risked cancer and birth defects. Vietnamese survivors and U.S. military personnel still suffer from the effects of their exposure to these poisonous chemicals.

## Sailors

U.S. Navy sailors played multiple roles in the Vietnam War. They served on ships and on aircraft carriers in the South China Sea. They also served on smaller boats that carried out missions on Vietnam's rivers and other waterways. Sailors on these smaller boats were able to travel deep into enemy-controlled territory. There, they worked to prevent supplies from reaching the Viet Cong.

Some sailors worked under the Navy's Military Sealift Command. These military personnel were responsible for delivering equipment, ammunition, vehicles, fuel, and weapons to U.S. forces via ports in South Vietnam. Other sailors were assigned to land duty, helping with the construction of military facilities in South Vietnam.

Some crewmembers on aircraft carriers were responsible for directing aircraft to and from the ship. Their work required precision and exceptional communication skills.

## Women in Vietnam

Approximately 11,000 military women were stationed in Vietnam during the war. Those serving as nurses took part in a brief basic training program before traveling to Vietnam with the Army Nurse Corps. Nurses often worked 12-hour shifts for six days per week. From March 1962 to March 1973, when the last Army nurses left Vietnam, some 5,000 served in the conflict. Five female Army nurses lost their lives during the war.

Other women arrived in Vietnam as members of the U.S. Women's Army Corps, while some were in the Air Force, Marines, and Navy. None of the women were assigned to combat roles, however. Most worked as air traffic controllers, clerks, and intelligence officers. Some women served in the Army Medical Specialist Corps, where they worked as dieticians, physical therapists, and occupational therapists.

Military nurses did more than treat U.S. troops. They also cared for Vietnamese citizens, including children, who were affected by the war.

Many of the military women sent to Vietnam had little preparation for the conditions they would face there. They learned how to deal with the violence and risk after they arrived.

# A Soldier's Uniform

## HELMET

U.S. Army soldiers and Marines wore the M1 Helmet. This was painted olive green and had a rolled edging. A camouflage cover was usually placed over the helmet. The cover had two sides, each with its own color pattern. Green camouflage was used in spring and summer. The beige pattern was used in fall and winter. Small holes in the cover allowed the soldier to add real leaves and branches to the helmet. The helmet weighed about 3.16 pounds (1.4 kg). It protected the wearer from flying **shrapnel** and glancing bullets, but did not stop a direct shot.

**S**oldiers heading to war were equipped with a standard uniform that they wore while on active duty in the field. Each soldier also had a kit that accompanied the uniform. The kit contained all the equipment the soldier was expected to need while away from his base of operations. The soldier carried his gear wherever he went. This is an example of the type of uniform worn by a U.S. infantry soldier during the Vietnam War.

## SHIRT AND JACKET

Due to the heat and humidity of Vietnam, ground soldiers were assigned uniforms that were lightweight and loose-fitting. An Army soldier's utility shirt was made from olive green cotton sateen. The utility shirt was usually worn over a white t-shirt and tucked into the soldier's trousers. A wind-resistant cotton jacket could be worn over the shirt. Four pockets on the front of the jacket were used to store ammunition and personal items.

## FOOTWEAR

Most ground soldiers wore the jungle, or tropical, combat boot when in the field. The boots had nylon ankle supports and reinforced soles. This was to protect soldiers if they accidentally stepped on the poisoned stakes or spikes sometimes used by the enemy in booby traps. Drainage eyelets on the boots allowed the soldier's feet to breathe and trapped moisture to escape.

## TROUSERS

Like the utility shirt, a soldier's utility trousers were made from olive green cotton sateen. Two hip pockets, as well as two patch pockets, were used to carry their survival kit and other small items. The bottom of each trouser leg had a drawstring that allowed the soldier to fasten the pant close to his leg.

## SUSPENDERS AND EQUIPMENT BELT

Soldiers used M1956 suspenders to carry their equipment. They did this by attaching their gear to a system of loops and hooks that ran along the suspender straps. A soldier's sleeping gear and first-aid kit could be connected to his suspenders, allowing him to have important supplies close at hand.

The suspenders were attached to an equipment belt that was worn around the waist. The belt had a series of eyelets that the soldier used to carry more equipment, including field packs, ammunition pouches, and canteen covers.

## FIELD PACK

A soldier carried larger items in his field pack. These packs came in several formats. The fanny pack could be attached to the suspenders by stringing the suspenders through two tabs located on top of the pack. Adaptor straps could be attached to a soldier's suspenders so that the pack could be worn higher on the back.

## CANTEEN

It was important for soldiers to stay hydrated in the heat of Vietnam. Each soldier was equipped with a canteen in which to carry water. The canteen was made of plastic and held 1 quart (1 liter) of liquid. Most soldiers carried at least two canteens at all times. One canteen was placed in a canvas bag and strapped onto the equipment belt so that the soldier had quick access to his water supply.

## AMMUNITION CASE

A soldier carried his gun ammunition in a small canvas bag. The bag was attached to the pistol belt for easy access. Two straps hung from each side of the ammunition case. This is where the soldier hung his supply of hand grenades.

# Vietnam Weapons

**B**oth the U.S. Navy and Air Force employed many different types of aircraft during the war. Pilots flew fighter planes in air battles against the enemy, while bombers launched full-scale attacks on enemy cities and military targets. Helicopters were used for observation, transport, and attack duties.

Since the Vietnam War consisted mainly of guerrilla warfare, both sides used landmines extensively to launch surprise attacks on the enemy. As well, military personnel carried grenades, rifles, and machine guns through the largely jungle terrain.

## MACHINE GUNS

The machine gun was one of the most highly valued weapons of the Vietnam War. U.S. troops relied mainly on the M60 machine gun, which could be used by ground forces or mounted onto a helicopter and fired from the air. The M60 allowed soldiers to fire a stream of rounds at the enemy in quick succession. It is estimated that the M60 could shoot 550 rounds per minute at distances up to 2,000 yards (1,829 meters).

## RIFLES

The M16A1 was the standard rifle of the U.S. military during the war. The lightweight assault rifle was capable of semi-automatic and fully automatic fire. In full-automatic mode, it could release up to 900 rounds per minute. Some M16A1 rifles were fitted with the M203 grenade launcher. This allowed the soldier to have a dual-purpose weapon. The grenade launcher could shoot its weapons 425 yards (389 meters).

## TANKS

Due to the soft jungle terrain of Vietnam, tanks played only a supporting role in the war. They provided cover fire for U.S. troops and guarded key roadways. U.S. forces relied mainly on the M48 Patton tank. The tank was equipped with mounted machine guns, as well as a turret gun that could rotate in all directions. The M48 carried a crew of four.

# AIRCRAFT

U.S. forces waged fierce battles in the skies over Vietnam. The AC-47 "Spooky" was a cargo plane converted into a gunship. The pilot's side of the aircraft was equipped with machine guns that fired through two rear window openings and the side cargo door. The pilot could control the guns either individually or together. The AC-47 was mostly used for close air support for U.S. ground troops. The aircraft could orbit an area for several hours, providing suppressing fire.

The Cessna A-37 Dragonfly light attack aircraft made its first appearance during the Vietnam War. Its main use was to provide air support by escorting helicopters and bombing enemy targets near battles. The Dragonfly was armed with high explosive bombs, cluster bombs, rockets, missiles, and machine guns.

# HELICOPTERS

The Vietnam War was the first conflict in which helicopters were used on a large scale by the armed forces. The United States' primary helicopter was the Bell UH-1 Iroquois. Nicknamed the Huey, the Bell UH-1 was armed with multi-barreled 7.62 mm Gatling guns, M60 machine guns, and rockets. These helicopters were used in a variety of ways. Their main role was transporting troops to and from the battlefield. They also performed search and rescue operations and were used for Medevac, or the medical evacuation, of wounded soldiers to hospitals.

# LAND MINES

The jungle environment made land mines an ideal weapon in the Vietnam War. Buried in the thick, leafy growth, they were difficult to see and easy to step on or drive over. One of the land mines used by U.S. forces was the M14, a mine about 2 inches (5 centimeters) wide. It carried only a small amount of explosive and was designed to harm only those people or objects that came into direct contact with it.

# Timeline

## The War Overseas

**August 1964**
After receiving reports that North Vietnamese forces have attacked destroyers in the Gulf of Tonkin, Congress passes the Gulf of Tonkin Resolution. The resolution leads to greater U.S. military involvement in Vietnam.

**November 3 to 22, 1967**
The Battle of Dak To is fought in Kon Tum Province. The Americans are successful in driving the North Vietnamese out of the area.

**March 1965**
The first U.S. combat troops officially arrive in South Vietnam. The United States also begins a bombing campaign in North Vietnam.

**November 14 to 18, 1965**
The Battle of Ia Drang takes place in the Central Highlands of South Vietnam. More than 300 U.S. troops die during the fighting.

## The War at Home

**November 1963**
Lyndon B. Johnson becomes president. Within his first year in office, he increases U.S. troop presence in Vietnam.

**March 1973**
The last U.S. combat soldiers leave South Vietnam, although some military advisors and Marines remain behind to protect U.S. installations.

**April 1975**
U.S. helicopters airlift more than 1,000 U.S. civilians and almost 7,000 South Vietnamese refugees out of Saigon. North Vietnamese forces capture Saigon on April 30, ending the war.

**January 31, 1968**
North Vietnam launches the Tet **Offensive**, attacking approximately 100 cities in South Vietnam. The communist forces are defeated and suffer heavy **casualties**. However, the United States harbors doubts that the war can be won. The first peace talks begin in the following months.

**March 1972**
The North Vietnamese launch an attack across the border in the Easter Offensive. They are eventually driven back by the South Vietnamese Army and remaining U.S. forces.

**March 1975**
North Vietnam launches a major attack against the South.

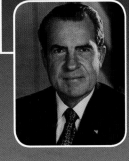

**July 1969**
President Nixon begins the withdrawal of U.S. troops. By early 1972, there are only about 130,000 U.S. military personnel still in South Vietnam.

**January 27, 1973**
The Paris Peace Accords are signed, ending U.S. involvement in the Vietnam War.

**March 1968**
President Johnson announces he will not run for re-election. Richard Nixon wins the vote in the fall election.

# American Battles

U.S. troops in Vietnam were mostly involved in a guerrilla war against the Viet Cong rather than in battles with the North Vietnamese army. The Viet Cong would launch hit-and-run attacks and then escape into the jungle. U.S. soldiers also faced **ambushes** and booby traps. As a result, there were very few formal battles during the war. However, those that did take place saw U.S. troops engaged in some of the bloodiest battles they had ever fought.

Vietnam's Central Highlands are located in the southwestern part of the country. The area borders Laos and Cambodia.

## The Battle of Ia Drang

The Battle of Ia Drang was fought from November 14 to 18, 1965. It took place in the Ia Drang Valley, in the Central Highlands of South Vietnam, and was the first major battle of the Vietnam War to involve U.S. troops.

The enemy had attacked a base in the area, and U.S. forces were keen to counterattack. However, they found it difficult to track down the enemy in the rugged landscape. It was felt that this problem could be overcome if troops were sent in by helicopter. The first troops were dropped into the X-Ray **landing zone** on November 14. Once on the ground, patrols soon located the enemy, meeting with heavy resistance. One **platoon** was driven back, and the other was soon surrounded by North Vietnamese forces. The Americans continued to fight, waiting for reinforcements to arrive.

### NOVEMBER 14

U.S. troops are dropped into the X-Ray landing zone to locate enemy forces. One U.S. platoon soon finds itself trapped by North Vietnamese forces.

### NOVEMBER 15

The platoon is rescued when air support and ground reinforcements arrive. After two days of fighting, U.S. troops begin heading to two other landing zones.

The next day, U.S. air support began firing on the enemy. They were able to drive the enemy back, but the U.S. troops took heavy losses, with 200 casualties. The platoon was finally rescued when ground reinforcements arrived from the Victor landing zone.

The Americans began to leave the area, trying to make their way to other landing zones. To cover the movement of the ground forces, B-52 Stratofortress bombers began attacking enemy positions. However, North Vietnamese forces ambushed the U.S. troops heading to the Albany landing zone. The Americans suffered major losses before reinforcements and air support arrived. The surprise attack at Albany was the deadliest ambush U.S. troops experienced during the entire war, with 155 U.S. military personnel losing their lives.

## The Battle of Ia Drang

Albany Landing Zone

Tango Landing Zone

X-Ray Landing Zone

Chu Pong Mountain

Victor Landing Zone

Yankee Landing Zone

Whiskey Landing Zone

### Legend
⭐ North Vietnamese Troops
🇺🇸 American Troops
➡ American Movements

## NOVEMBER 17

North Vietnamese forces ambush one group of U.S. troops. By the time reinforcements arrive, 155 soldiers die, and another 124 are wounded.

## NOVEMBER 18

The Americans spend the day taking stock of their losses. They are flown out of the area the next day.

## The Battle of Dak To

The Battle of Dak To was fought from November 3 to 22, 1967. Over the course of the previous summer, the North Vietnamese had launched attacks in Kon Tum Province, near the border between South Vietnam, Cambodia, and Laos. U.S. forces fought some enemy units, but the North Vietnamese soon withdrew from the area. In early October, however, the United States learned that the enemy was moving back into Kon Tum. The United States began dropping troops into the area on November 3 and quickly found that the North Vietnamese had established strong defenses on the hills around Dak To.

The North Vietnamese decision to attack the Dak To airstrip was strategic. The airport was used to transport U.S. troops inland to the battlefield.

In the subsequent three weeks, the Americans attacked the North Vietnamese positions with massive air and artillery strikes. The North Vietnamese returned fire, doing what damage they could before retreating to the safety of the jungle. A key focus of North Vietnamese artillery attack was the U.S. airstrip at Dak To. On November 15, several aircraft were destroyed, and the base's fuel and ammunition depots were blown up.

### NOVEMBER 3

Upon hearing that the North Vietnamese was moving into the hills of Kon Tum province, the United States sends its troops in to push them back.

### NOVEMBER 15

North Vietnamese forces destroy several U.S. aircraft, as well as the base's fuel and ammunition supplies, at the Dak To airstrip.

On November 19, U.S. troops attacked Hill 875, one of the three main battle fronts. They became caught in an ambush and were surrounded. Air support was called in but had little effect on the hillside's dense jungle. One of the worst **friendly fire** incidents of the Vietnam War occurred when a U.S. aircraft bombed the hill, killing 42 men and wounding 45. Reinforcements arrived, and on November 21, the **battalion** was able to advance to the crest of Hill 875. After two days of close-quarters fighting, the hill was finally captured.

Once the North Vietnamese were driven out of Kon Tum Province, U.S. forces turned their attention to the border areas. This left other parts of the country vulnerable, and set the stage for the Tet Offensive against the cities of South Vietnam in early 1968.

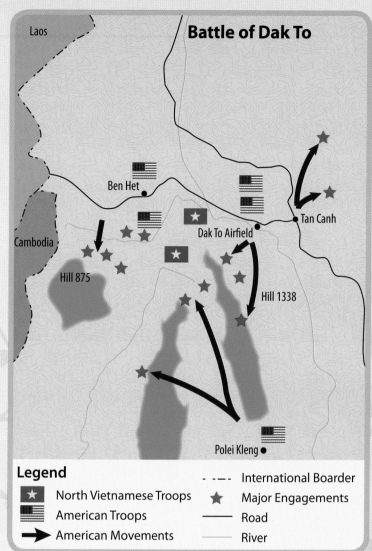

**Battle of Dak To**

Laos
Ben Het
Cambodia
Dak To Airfield
Tan Canh
Hill 875
Hill 1338
Polei Kleng

**Legend**

- ⭐ North Vietnamese Troops
- 🇺🇸 American Troops
- ➡️ American Movements
- - ⋅ - ⋅ - International Boarder
- ⭐ Major Engagements
- —— Road
- —— River

## NOVEMBER 19

A U.S. Airborne battalion attacks Hill 875, a North Vietnamese stronghold. They are ambushed by North Vietnamese forces and then bombed by their own troops.

## NOVEMBER 21

After reaching the crest of Hill 875 on November 21, the United States engages in two days of fighting. By November 23, they have secured Hill 875.

## The Battle of Hue

The Battle of Hue was part of the Tet Offensive launched on January 31, 1968. The conflict lasted for 26 days and was one of the longest and bloodiest battles of the Vietnam War. Two U.S. Army battalions and three U.S. Marine battalions supported the South Vietnamese army against more than 12,000 North Vietnamese and Viet Cong soldiers.

Many of the buildings inside the Imperial City were destroyed during the battle. One building that remains, however, is Ngo Mon Gate, the city's main entrance.

The Tet Offensive was the largest military operation by either side up to that point in the war. On the first day of the Vietnamese New Year, known as Tet, the North Vietnamese Army and Viet Cong attacked many cities and towns, U.S. bases, and even the South Vietnamese capital, Saigon.

The city of Hue is very close to the border between North and South Vietnam. During the war, Hue was a base for U.S. supply boats and was close to an important river and road link. Despite its key location, the city was poorly defended. In the early morning hours of January 31, North Vietnamese forces advanced into the city, planning to take control of the Imperial Citadel—a key military installation for the South Vietnamese army—and the U.S. air base south of Hue. By 8:00 a.m., they had raised the Viet Cong flag over the Citadel. By the end of the day, they occupied most of the city.

The South Vietnamese army counterattacked to recapture the Citadel and clear the north bank of the river. U.S. Army units moved to the west side of Hue to stop North Vietnamese reinforcements from moving farther into the city. In the meantime, U.S. forces were also engaging the enemy south of the river, trying to stop the advance to the air base.

## JANUARY 31

At about 2:00 a.m., North Vietnamese forces advance on the city of Hue. They lay claim to the Imperial Citadel by 8:00 a.m. and occupy most of the city by the end of the day.

## FEBRUARY 4

U.S. Marines begin routing out the enemy, building by building. U.S. Navy ships located offshore support the ground effort by firing on the city.

On February 4, Marines began house-to-house fighting to drive the enemy out of the city. They were supported by gunfire from Navy ships offshore. By February 9, the south bank had been cleared. House-to-house fighting continued as the city was retaken one block at a time. The enemy was finally forced out of Hue on February 27.

The Battle of Hue was a victory for the United States and South Vietnam, but was achieved at a heavy cost. U.S. casualties were in excess of 1,500. South Vietnamese forces had more than 2,200 casualties. At least 5,000 civilians are also believed to have died in the battle.

The bitter fighting in Hue and in other parts of the country during the Tet Offensive had an effect back in the United States. As anti-war sentiments continued to grow, the U.S. government began to think about withdrawing U.S. forces from Vietnam.

Ordinary citizens did what they could to escape the violence in their city. When bridges were destroyed, they used small boats to get across the river and out of Hue.

## FEBRUARY 23

After securing the city's south bank on February 9, U.S. forces continue clearing the city. On February 23, they drive the enemy out of the Imperial Citadel.

## FEBRUARY 27

The fighting ends. All sides have experienced heavy losses. Hue is left in shambles, with more than 80 percent of the city damaged or destroyed.

# Heroic Americans

The men and women who fought in the Vietnam War came from a range of backgrounds. They were united by a desire to fight for their country. While all performed heroic acts, as the war progressed, some names became better known than others. Some soldiers were hailed for their bravery and strong leadership. Others were celebrated because they performed feats unlike anyone else.

## COLIN POWELL
## (1937– )

Colin Powell was born in New York, on April 5, 1937. After high school, Powell joined the Reserve Officers' Training Corps (ROTC), a college program that trains officers for the military. He graduated in 1958 and became a second lieutenant in the U.S. Army. After rising to the rank of captain, Powell became an advisor to the South Vietnamese Army, holding this position from 1962 to 1963. He was wounded while on patrol in an area held by the Viet Cong and returned to the United States.

By the time Powell went back to Vietnam in 1968, he had been promoted to the rank of major. His second tour of duty in Vietnam ended when he was in a helicopter crash. Powell was awarded the Soldier's Medal for his heroism after he pulled his comrades from the burning wreckage.

After the war, Powell worked in different government departments in Washington, D.C. and became National Security Advisor in 1987. Two years later, he was appointed as Chairman of the Joint Chiefs of Staff. This made Powell the highest-ranking officer in the U.S. Armed Forces and the main military advisor to the president. Powell was the first, and so far only, African American to hold this position. Powell retired from the military in 1993. He served as Secretary of State under President George W. Bush from 2000 to 2005.

# JOHN MCCAIN
## (1936– )

John McCain was born on August 29, 1936. McCain's father and grandfather were both admirals in the U.S. Navy. Following in their footsteps, McCain entered the U.S. Naval Academy and trained as a pilot after graduation. During the Vietnam War, he was assigned to aircraft carrier duty, serving on the USS *Forrestal* and USS *Oriskany*. On a bombing mission over North Vietnam in 1967, McCain's plane was shot down. Seriously injured in the crash, McCain was captured and became a prisoner of war (POW). He was freed in 1973, but his war wounds left him with lifelong physical disabilities.

McCain entered politics in 1976, when he was assigned as the Navy's liaison to the Senate. He then went on to serve in the U.S. House of Representatives and the Senate. He ran for the Republican presidential nomination in 2000, but lost to eventual winner George W. Bush. In 2008, McCain was the Republican candidate for president, but lost the election to Barack Obama. John McCain is currently the U.S. senator from Arizona.

# JOHN KERRY
## (1943– )

John Kerry was born in Aurora, Colorado, on December 11, 1943. After graduating from Yale University in 1966, he joined the Naval Reserve. Kerry served in Vietnam from 1968 to 1969. He was the officer in charge of a patrol craft fast, also known as a swift boat. Kerry and his five-man crew ferried soldiers and supplies into areas controlled by the enemy. He was wounded during his service and was awarded medals for bravery, including the Bronze Star, Silver Star, and three Purple Hearts. Upon his return to the United States, Kerry became a spokesperson for an anti-war group called Vietnam Veterans Against the War. He made speeches and gave interviews to the media criticizing how the United States was fighting the war in Vietnam.

Kerry later entered politics and was elected as the U.S. senator from Massachusetts in 1984. He was the Democratic candidate for president in 2004, but narrowly lost the election to George W. Bush. In 2013, he replaced Hillary Rodham Clinton as the country's Secretary of State.

# The Home Front

At first, it seemed like the war in Vietnam would have little effect on everyday life in the United States. The fighting was a long way from home, and many people supported President Johnson's decision to send in troops in March 1965. The situation changed, however, as the United States became more involved in Vietnam. The war was covered extensively in the media, so people back home were able to see the brutality of what was happening. Opposition to U.S. involvement in Vietnam grew, leading to demonstrations all over the country.

## The War in the Media

The Vietnam War was widely covered on television and in newspapers and magazines. It was, in fact, the first war to be televised. Every day, television newscasts showed images of dead and wounded U.S. soldiers and relayed the horrors of war. Unlike previous wars, the government could not glorify the war or use **propaganda** to make the fighting seem noble. The war effort at home suffered as people did not want to contribute to an event that was taking lives in such a violent manner.

Even though these reports showed the reality of Vietnam, journalists often expressed their own views on the war in their reporting. As these reports shaped the opinions of everyday Americans at home, the U.S. government began accusing journalists of helping the enemy. Government officials argued that U.S. reporting was exaggerating the damage the North Vietnamese were inflicting on the south. They felt that U.S. journalists were trying to force the government to take its troops out of the war. Journalists, on the other hand, argued that they were only reflecting the public's changing views on the conduct of the war.

Television networks sent their top journalists, including Walter Cronkite, to cover the Vietnam War.

To counter the anti-draft protests, people who supported the draft organized parades and other events to promote their readiness to fight.

## The Draft

To ensure a ready supply of troops for the war, the United States enacted compulsory military service, also known as the draft, for males between the ages of 18 and 26. As the war progressed, the government started calling up more men to the armed forces. Protests against the draft began in 1965 and steadily grew stronger as the war progressed.

Many men ripped or burned their draft cards as a form of protest.

Many men found loopholes in the draft act that allowed them to avoid military service. Some **draft-dodgers**, for instance, enrolled in university or married because students and married men were exempt from the draft. Others joined national reserve forces, such as the Coast Guard or National Guard. In doing this, they were able to remain in the U.S. and avoid the draft. Some men escaped the draft by leaving the United States entirely. They moved to Mexico as well as several European countries. About 30,000 men went to live in Canada.

## The Anti-War Movement

Anti-war protests were a regular occurrence during the war. Most took place on college campuses and in major cities. On October 21, 1967, about 100,000 people protested at the Lincoln Memorial in Washington, D.C. Almost 35,000 of the protestors marched to the Pentagon later that day, and hundreds of people were arrested. Two years later, on November 15, 1969, Washington was the scene of another demonstration when more than 500,000 Americans gathered for the largest anti-war protest in U.S. history.

Several Hollywood stars joined the anti-war movement. Actress Jane Fonda was a vocal opponent of the war, participating in numerous demonstrations and, at one point, paying a visit to North Vietnam.

The most violent anti-war protest occurred at Ohio's Kent State University on May 4, 1970. The National Guard was trying to control the event when guardsmen shot into the crowd. Four students were killed, and ten were wounded. The shooting led to even more demonstrations all over the country. Protests against the war continued until the end of U.S. involvement in 1973.

The violence at Kent State led other universities, including the University of New Mexico, to form their own protests. These demonstrations often led to military intervention as well.

## American Politics

The Vietnam War had a great effect on the U.S. political scene. President Johnson had become very unpopular by the time of the presidential election in 1968. At the end of March, Johnson announced that he would not run for re-election. Hubert Humphrey won the Democratic nomination, but he led a party that had lost the respect of the U.S. people. He was defeated by Republican candidate Richard Nixon in the presidential election.

Hubert Humphrey had been President Johnson's vice president before running for president himself.

Nixon took immediate steps to end U.S. involvement in the war. He began to withdraw troops from Vietnam and continued peace negotiations. Nixon was re-elected in 1972, and the last U.S. combat troops left Vietnam in 1973.

Richard Nixon campaigned on a promise to end U.S. involvement in the Vietnam War. This promise contributed greatly to his win in the 1968 election.

# The War Comes to an End

**R**ichard Nixon saw that the United States was fighting a losing battle in Vietnam. He felt the best course of action was to withdraw U.S. troops from Vietnam and let the South Vietnamese fight the war themselves. This plan was called Vietnamization, and U.S. troops began leaving Vietnam in July 1969. However, even while trying to negotiate a peace deal with North Vietnam, the United States continued to supply South Vietnam with military equipment and support them in the fight against the communists.

In 1971, the South Vietnamese Army launched an attack on the neighboring country of Laos, where the Viet Cong and North Vietnamese had established military bases and supply routes. The United States did not supply ground troops, but supported the South Vietnamese campaign with aircraft and helicopters. The attack was a failure and showed that, without U.S. support, South Vietnam was not likely to survive.

In March 1972, North Vietnam launched a massive attack across the border, called the Easter Offensive. The North Vietnamese were eventually driven back by the South Vietnamese Army, but only with the help of U.S. air power. Once again, it seemed clear that South Vietnam would not be able to continue the war without U.S. support.

When South Vietnamese soldiers moved toward the Laos border, their goal was to destroy Ho Chi Minh Trail. This pathway system began in North Vietnam and went through Laos, before arriving at the South Vietnam border. It was a main route for the transfer of arms between the North Vietnam military and the Viet Cong.

On January 27, 1973, the Paris Peace Accords were finally signed after years of negotiations. This agreement officially ended U.S. involvement in Vietnam. American POWs were released, and the last U.S. combat soldiers left South Vietnam the following March. Some U.S. military advisors and Marines stayed in the country to protect U.S. installations.

The U.S. military took extreme measures to help people escape Saigon before it fell.

A ceasefire was declared throughout Vietnam, but fighting soon broke out again. The United States supplied South Vietnam with weapons and military equipment to help defend the country. However, the U.S. government would not approve any more bombing raids to help South Vietnam if the North attacked.

In 1974, Gerald Ford replaced Nixon as president. U.S. support for South Vietnam was greatly reduced as the war continued. In March 1975, North Vietnam launched a final major attack against the south. By April 27, Saigon was surrounded by enemy forces. Two days later, U.S. helicopters began Operation Frequent Wind, evacuating people from Saigon and flying them out of the city to U.S. aircraft carriers off the coast. In the early hours of April 30, the last Marines left the U.S. embassy by helicopter. North Vietnamese forces finally captured Saigon on April 30. In 1976, the north and the south were officially reunited as the Socialist Republic of Vietnam.

The U.S. government sent Henry Kissinger, its National Security Advisor, to France as its main negotiator during the Paris Peace talks.

# The Aftermath

The Vietnam War left the United States in conflict with itself. Its reputation as a world leader was compromised by the fact that it had been unable to defeat the enemy and bring the war to an end. U.S. citizens had lost respect for their government. They also did not know how to react to the soldiers who returned home. Many soldiers, on the other hand, did not know how to respond to a country that had not supported their efforts in Vietnam.

## The U.S. Military

The United States had seen itself as the defender of freedom and democracy against the threat of communism all around the world. The military had also seemed invincible after its victories in World War II and Korea. The defeat in Vietnam was a humiliation for the military, and it took many years for the armed forces to recover from it. The loss was also a major blow to U.S. pride in the Cold War against communist powers.

For many years after the Vietnam War, the U.S. military was wary of getting involved in international conflicts and reluctant to do anything that would damage its reputation on the national level. Shortly after the war ended, the government rescinded the draft, and the U.S. Armed Forces became a professional volunteer army.

Many Americans have compared the current War in Afghanistan to the Vietnam War in terms of duration and cost, both human and financial. The U.S. government is sensitive to these concerns and has made a commitment to remove its combat troops from Afghanistan by 2014.

## The U.S. Public

The war had deeply divided people in the United States, and the defeat led to a loss of pride and self-confidence. Americans blamed the government for the war, the defeat, and the state in which it left the country. The Vietnam War had cost the country more than $120 billion at the time. This spending had long-term effects on the U.S. economy. As the war drew to a close, people learned that the United States had not always acted honorably in Vietnam. They discovered that U.S. troops had been responsible for the killing of hundreds of civilians and that the authorities had conspired to hide the information. Americans trusted the government and their leaders much less after the war.

Over time, people have begun to understand the conditions U.S. troops experienced in Vietnam and express gratitude for the efforts they made.

## Vietnam Veterans

U.S. military personnel returning from the war came home to a country that viewed them as an embarrassment. Veterans were not treated as heroes, and there were no parades welcoming them home. Some people saw veterans as murderers of civilians. Others blamed them because the United States lost the war.

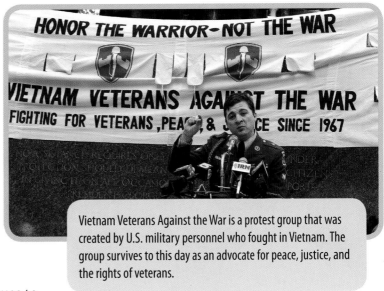

Vietnam Veterans Against the War is a protest group that was created by U.S. military personnel who fought in Vietnam. The group survives to this day as an advocate for peace, justice, and the rights of veterans.

The veterans had personal issues to deal with as well. Some were able to easily transition back into their lives. Others, however, came back physically or psychologically wounded. Many veterans were unable to find employment because of their perceived role in the war. They became bitter at the way they were treated. Slowly, Americans came to accept that Vietnam veterans had been good soldiers in a bad war.

# By The Numbers

## Men and Women

Men made up the majority of military personnel serving in Vietnam. Over the course of the war, almost 3.4 million men were sent to Vietnam. The number of women, at 11,000, was much smaller. However, while many of the men were drafted, the women volunteered for service.

**3.4 Million Men**

**11,000 Women**

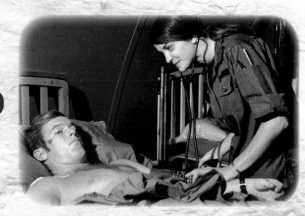

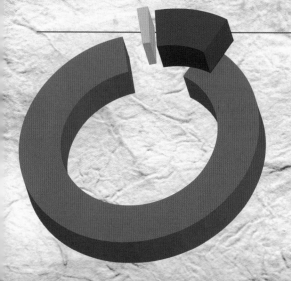

## Ethnic Backgrounds

The Vietnam War was the first war in which men of all ethnic backgrounds fought together. Previously, ethnic minorities, specifically African Americans, were placed in segregated units. Other minorities that served included Latin and Asian Americans.

- **88.4%** Caucasian
- **10.6%** African-American
- **1.0%** Other

# B-52 Missions

The B-52 bomber played a key role in air attacks over Vietnam. As the war progressed, the number of bombing missions increased, jumping to more than 10,000 per year. In 1968 alone, more than 20,000 missions were flown, with approximately 26 tons (23.5 tonnes) worth of bombs released per mission.

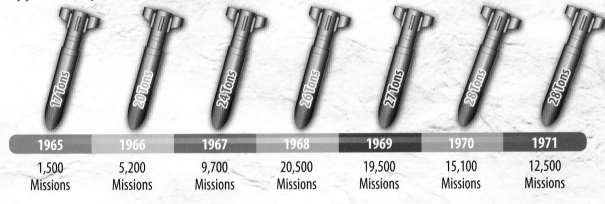

| 1965 | 1966 | 1967 | 1968 | 1969 | 1970 | 1971 |
|------|------|------|------|------|------|------|
| 1,500 Missions | 5,200 Missions | 9,700 Missions | 20,500 Missions | 19,500 Missions | 15,100 Missions | 12,500 Missions |

# U.S. Defense Spending

The Vietnam War was an expensive endeavor for the United States government. This chart shows the percentage of gross domestic product (GDP) the country spent on the war effort. GDP is the total amount of goods and services a country produces over a year. In the early stages of the Vietnam War, approximately 10 percent of the United States' GDP was being put toward defense spending. This percentage is double the amount spent on the current war in Afghanistan.

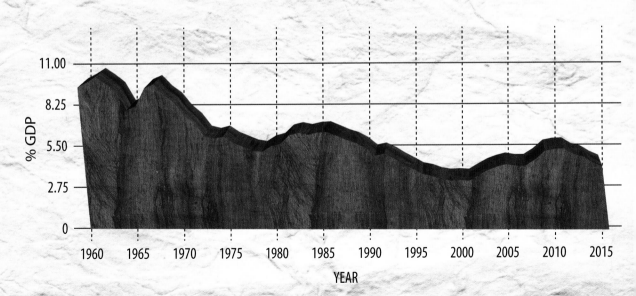

# War Casualties

The conflict in Vietnam not only took a toll on the United States and Vietnam, but the countries surrounding Vietnam as well. In many cases, these countries were not directly involved in the war. They became caught in the crossfire when the battles came across their borders. It is estimated that the war took the lives of about 1.4 million soldiers. The war also claimed the lives of many civilians. It is estimated that at least 600,000 Vietnamese civilians died during the war.

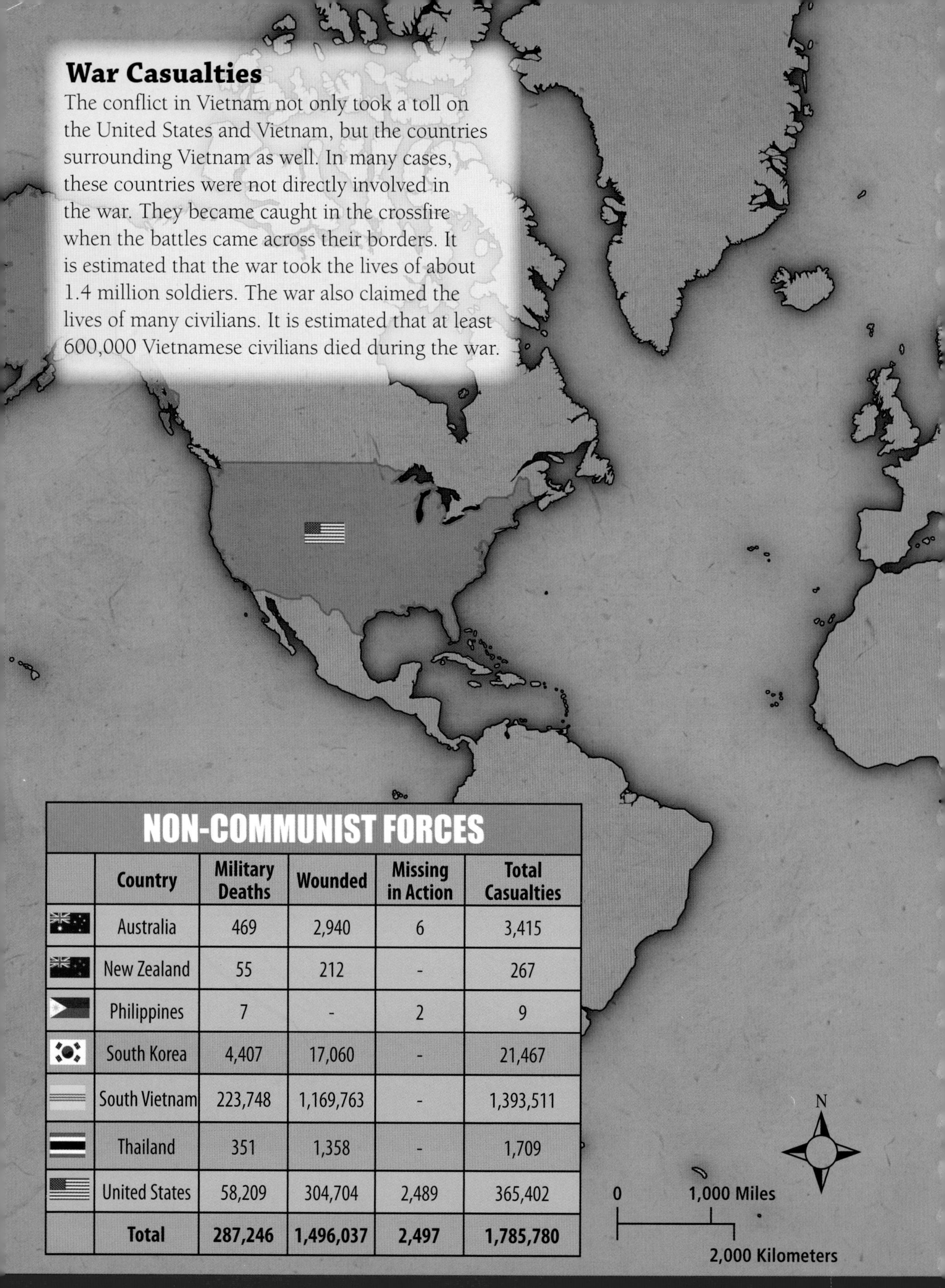

## NON-COMMUNIST FORCES

| | Country | Military Deaths | Wounded | Missing in Action | Total Casualties |
|---|---|---|---|---|---|
| | Australia | 469 | 2,940 | 6 | 3,415 |
| | New Zealand | 55 | 212 | - | 267 |
| | Philippines | 7 | - | 2 | 9 |
| | South Korea | 4,407 | 17,060 | - | 21,467 |
| | South Vietnam | 223,748 | 1,169,763 | - | 1,393,511 |
| | Thailand | 351 | 1,358 | - | 1,709 |
| | United States | 58,209 | 304,704 | 2,489 | 365,402 |
| | **Total** | **287,246** | **1,496,037** | **2,497** | **1,785,780** |

0          1,000 Miles

2,000 Kilometers

## COMMUNIST FORCES

| | Country | Military Deaths | Wounded | Missing in Action | Total Casualties |
|---|---|---|---|---|---|
| | China | 1,446 | 4,200 | - | 5,646 |
| | North Vietnam | 1,100,000 | 600,000 | - | 1,700,000 |
| | Soviet Union | 16 | - | - | 16 |
| | **Total** | **1,101,462** | **604,200** | **-** | **1,705,662** |

# How We Remember

The Vietnam War affected families all across the country. While initially reluctant to acknowledge the war, people eventually began to understand the sacrifices made by U.S. troops. There was a movement to honor those who had fought, those who had been injured, and those who had died throughout the course of the war.

## VIETNAM VETERANS MEMORIAL WALL

The Vietnam Veterans Memorial Wall is part of the larger Vietnam Veterans Memorial, located in Washington, D.C. Completed in 1982, the wall is the main part of the memorial. It is made up of two black granite walls that are 246 feet, 8 inches (75 m) long. Each wall is engraved with the names of those U.S. soldiers who did not return from the war. As of 2011, 58,272 names were listed. A diamond beside a name indicates that the person was killed, while a cross indicates that the person is missing.

## THE THREE SERVICEMEN

The Three Servicemen statue is part of the Vietnam Veterans Memorial. It is located near the west entrance to the Memorial Wall. Sometimes called The Three Soldiers, the bronze statue portrays three figures dressed in uniforms and gear used by members of the U.S. military during the Vietnam War. It was decided that the statue should accurately represent the major U.S. ethnic groups who served in the U.S. armed forces during the war. Thus, the three men are shown as Caucasian, African American, and Hispanic.

## VIETNAM WOMEN'S MEMORIAL

The Vietnam Women's Memorial was added to the Vietnam Veterans Memorial site in 1993. Located south of the Memorial Wall, it is dedicated to the U.S. women who served their country in the war. The statue portrays three uniformed women and a wounded soldier. One of the women looks to the sky while another one kneels, looking down in despair. The third woman tends to the wounded soldier. The memorial stands more than 6 feet (2 m) tall. It reminds visitors of the very important role women play in times of war.

In the decades after the war, memorials and other symbols of remembrance began to appear across the country and in the country where the war was fought. Some were local monuments, developed by individual communities to honor veterans. Others were created on behalf of the entire United States. Today, these memorials and symbols continue to pay tribute to those who served in the Vietnam War.

## THE MOVING WALL MEMORIAL

The Moving Wall Memorial was created so that people across the United States could experience the power of the Washington memorial. The memorial consists of two half-scale replicas of the Vietnam Veterans Memorial. They measure 250 feet (76 m) long and are 4 to 6 feet (1.2 to 1.8 m) high. Made of aluminum, they are engraved with the names of the more than 58,000 soldiers who died or went missing during the war. The displays tour the country between the months of April and November. They are set up in parks and other public spaces for people to view.

## VIETNAMESE-AMERICAN PEACE PARK

The Vietnamese-American Peace Park is located near the village of Bac Giang, in what was once North Vietnam. The idea for the park was developed in 1993 by two Vietnam veterans, one from each side of the conflict. The park was created as a symbol of peace and reconciliation. It features an orchard of plum, banyan, and lychee trees. These trees have been planted by war veterans from both sides. Over time, there are plans to build a museum on the site to reflect on the war and the price paid by everyone involved.

## MY LAI PEACE PARK

Following in the path of the Vietnamese-American Peace Park, the My Lai Peace Park was created in 1998, on the 30th anniversary of the My Lai Massacre, in which U.S. troops killed more than 300 Vietnamese civilians. The park is intended to be a place where people can engage in quiet reflection about the past and hope for a better future. It covers about 4 acres (2 hectares) and features trees, flower gardens, ponds, and a variety of shrubs. Several groups contribute to the park's maintenance, including anti-war supporters and local Vietnamese residents.

# Test Yourself

## MIX 'n MATCH

1. Bombing campaign
2. The U.S. president who ended the war
3. Chemical warfare
4. The Three Servicemen Statue
5. Main U.S. rifle in Vietnam
6. Anti-war protest
7. President of the United States 1963 to 1969

a. Lyndon Johnson
b. M16A1 Rifle
c. Richard Nixon
d. Kent State
e. Agent Orange
f. Operation Rolling Thunder
g. Washington, D.C.

## TRUE OR FALSE

1. The United States saw the Vietnam War as a fight against communism.
2. The M1 helmet protected a soldier from direct hits by bullets.
3. The Vietnam Veterans Memorial Wall is made of black marble.
4. Senator John McCain was held in North Vietnam as a prisoner of war.
5. Friendly fire killed more than 40 U.S. troops during the Battle of Dak To.
6. The Bell UH-1 Iroquois helicopter was nicknamed the Huey.
7. The Paris Peace Accords brought the Vietnam War to an end.
8. More than 58,000 Americans died or went missing during the Vietnam War.

# MULTIPLE CHOICE

1. In what year did the first U.S. combat troops officially arrive in Vietnam?
   a. 1950
   b. 1965
   c. 1968
   d. 1973

2. Which two countries were the main supporters of North Vietnam?
   a. United States and Soviet Union
   b. Great Britain and France
   c. France and Japan
   d. Soviet Union and China

3. Vietnam was a colony of which country prior to World War II?
   a. United States
   b. Japan
   c. France
   d. Great Britain

4. Who were the guerilla fighters that U.S. Forces battled during the war?
   a. Viet Minh
   b. Viet Cong
   c. Dien Bien Phu
   d. Tet

5. Approximately how many women served in the U.S. military in Vietnam?
   a. 7,000
   b. 4,500
   c. 11,000
   d. 14,000

6. What was the name of the attack launched by North Vietnam in January 1968?
   a. Tet Offensive
   b. Gulf of Tonkin Resolution
   c. Operation Frequent Wind
   d. Easter Offensive

7. Which president began the withdrawal of U.S. forces from Vietnam?
   a. Lyndon B. Johnson
   b. John F. Kennedy
   c. Gerald Ford
   d. Richard Nixon

Answers:
Mix and Match
1. f 2. c 3. e 4. g 5. b 6. d 7. a
True or False
1. True 2. False 3. False 4. True 5. True 6. True 7. False 8. True
Multiple choice: 1. b 2. d 3. c 4. b 5. c 6. a 7. d

# Key Words

**ally:** a person or group who is associated with another for a common purpose

**ambushes:** surprise attacks

**artillery:** large-caliber weapons, such as cannons and missile launchers

**battalion:** a military unit comprising 300 to 1,200 soldiers. Several battalions usually form a regiment or a brigade.

**casualties:** people who have been killed, taken prisoner, or are missing in action. Some battles also include the wounded among casualty figures.

**civilians:** people who are not active members of the armed forces

**Civil Rights Act:** laws prohibiting discrimination and segregation based on race in public places, employment, and voting

**Cold War:** the conflict between the United States and the Soviet Union after World War II

**colonial rule:** relating to colonies, or areas that remain under the control of another country

**communists:** people who believe in a system where, in theory, all people enjoy equal social and economic status

**democratic:** pertaining to a form of government in which the supreme power is vested in the people and exercised directly by them or by their elected agents

**dictators:** people who rule absolutely and oppressively

**draft dodgers:** people who evade compulsory military service

**empire:** a grouping of people and land under the rule of a sovereign state

**friendly fire:** attacks against the enemy that accidentally hit friendly forces

**guerilla war:** battles featuring irregular warfare, usually involving a member of an independent unit carrying out sabotage

**Indochina:** the name formerly used for Cambodia, Laos, and Vietnam

**infantry:** an army consisting of soldiers who fight on foot

**landing zone:** a place set aside for landing aircraft

**offensive:** an attack launched by military forces against the enemy

**platoon:** a subdivision of a company of troops

**propaganda:** information, ideas, or rumors deliberately spread to help or harm a person, group, or nation

**regime change:** when one country tries to get rid of another country's government, especially through force, and replace it with a government that supports its own interests

**shrapnel:** fragments from artillery fire

**Soviet Union:** a large country in eastern Europe and northern Asia from 1922 to 1991, comprising Russia and 14 other republics. Most of the territory is now known as Russia.

# Index

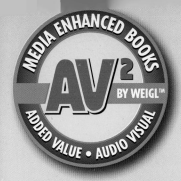

# Log on to www.av2books.com

AV² by Weigl brings you media enhanced books that support active learning. Go to www.av2books.com, and enter the special code found on page 2 of this book. You will gain access to enriched and enhanced content that supplements and complements this book. Content includes video, audio, weblinks, quizzes, a slide show, and activities.

## AV² Online Navigation

**Book Pages**
AV² pages directly correspond to pages in the book.

**Key Words**
Study vocabulary, and complete a matching word activity.

**Quizzes**
Test your knowledge.

**Slide Show**
View images and captions, and prepare a presentation.

**Audio**
Listen to sections of the book read aloud.

**Video**
Watch informative video clips.

**Embedded Weblinks**
Gain additional information for research.

**Try This!**
Complete activities and hands-on experiments.

---

AV² was built to bridge the gap between print and digital. We encourage you to tell us what you like and what you want to see in the future.

## Sign up to be an AV² Ambassador at www.av2books.com/ambassador.